Warriors Of The Light!

By Dancing Dove

Copyright 2015 Mary Bennett

Mary Bennett aka Dancing Dove

Table of Contents

Introduction
A note to the Warriors
A Warriors Prayer
The Good Fight
The Mighty Little Warrior
What Time is It? ; Raising Warriors of Faith
Dancing in Glory
Behold! Our Victory is Nigh!
Who Are We Following?
Emanating Light!
The Edge! ; The Lifter of My Head!
A Higher Calling!
Lead Them! ; For All of the Pain of Life Unfair
You Are Not a Door-mat! ; I Can Do All Things Through Him!
The Work of My Hands! ; Sometimes You Will Have to Dance Alone
The Spirit Came Down; The Sacred Feather
Resting
Where Does Your Help Come From?
What Darkness?
Bricks of Struggle
Are We There Yet, Dad? ; Burying Injustice
What We Bury . . .
How Long, O Lord? ; Hardened
Don't Give Up!
Wounded Pride
Watch and Wait! ; Warriors on a Mission
To Whom is the Arm of the LORD Revealed?
A Rock and a Hard Place; Night Watch
Purpose

Why Can't We Fly?
The POWER of HIS NAME!
My God Stands Guard! ; Foot-prints
Wounded Warrior; Tears for the Mortar
Thy Rod and Thy Staff
Division in the Ranks
Are We Walking in The Light?
Children of the Red Earth Gather
In My Human-ness
There's a Storm a 'brewing...; Borrowed Robes
Thieves in Our Midst
Cry Babies!
The Fruit of the Vine
Power Struggle.............
Forget Us Not!
Into The Light . . .

Warriors of The Light!

Why is this life such a struggle? It never seemed to be this much of a struggle before I found new life in Christ. Why now? Shouldn't my faith in Him make life easier?

We are in a battle ground for the very faith which we profess! The enemy is shrewd, he comes in as gently as a lamb to deceive and rob us blind! To take our eyes off of our Creator, and put it back in the flesh . . . wherein is death! We must contend for our faith! This battle ground is real! But the enemy has been defeated!

Perhaps in my sharing this collection of poetry we will all see that truly, we are not all so different! We fight the same battles, day in and day out! We feel alone, and unworthy – just as the enemy plans it! But no! This is far from the truth, for through Christ we are more than overcomers!

Warriors! Let us be salt and light together! A'ho!

~ Dancing Dove

Finally, my brethren, be strong in the Lord, and in the power of his might. Put on the whole armour of God, that ye may be able to stand against the wiles of the devil. For we wrestle not against flesh and blood, but against principalities, against powers, against the rulers of the darkness of this world, against spiritual wickedness in high places. Wherefore take unto you the whole armour of God, that ye may be able to withstand in the evil day, and having done all, to stand. Stand therefore, having your loins girt about with truth, and having on the breastplate of righteousness; And your feet shod with the preparation of the gospel of peace; Above all, taking the shield of faith, wherewith ye shall be able to quench all the fiery darts of the wicked. And take the helmet of salvation, and the sword of the Spirit, which is the word of God: Praying always with all prayer and supplication in the Spirit, and watching thereunto with all perseverance and supplication for all saints; And for me, that utterance may be given unto me, that I may open my mouth boldly, to make known the mystery of the gospel, For which I am an ambassador in bonds: that therein I may speak boldly, as I ought to speak.

My Warriors,

Don't get too comfortable!
Feeling like the black sheep?
Welcome to My world!
They didn't have the time of day for Me,
And they will not have the time of day for you!
Get used to it!
Hang in there, I'm preparing a place for you,
And I'll come and take you there
When it is ready!
But for now – stay strong –
And stay together!
Doing the right thing
Is not the most popular!
Just remember one thing,
I am with you always!
Now go.......
People are dying!
Be Salt and Light!

Love,

Your Creator!

And she brought forth her firstborn son, and wrapped him in swaddling clothes, and laid him in a manger; because there was no room for them in the inn. And Jesus saith unto him, The foxes have holes, and the birds of the air have nests; but the Son of man hath not where to lay his head.

If the world hate you, ye know that it hated me before it hated you.

"Go therefore and make disciples of all the nations, baptizing them in the name of the Father and the Son and the Holy Spirit, teaching them to observe all that I commanded you; and lo, I am with you always, even to the end of the age."

A Warriors Prayer:

Creator,

Help me to communicate Your Truth!
No matter what is needed, my life use!
Help me not to just make an empty sound,
But with love to share Your message all around!
Some have no ears, Creator!
Some have no eyes to see!
Help me reach the masses for You!
Creator, here am I! Send me!
Through me YOU can open up the deaf ears!
Through me YOU can open blinded eyes!
Through me YOU can enter darkened corners
And reach out to those who cry!

Always,

Your Warrior

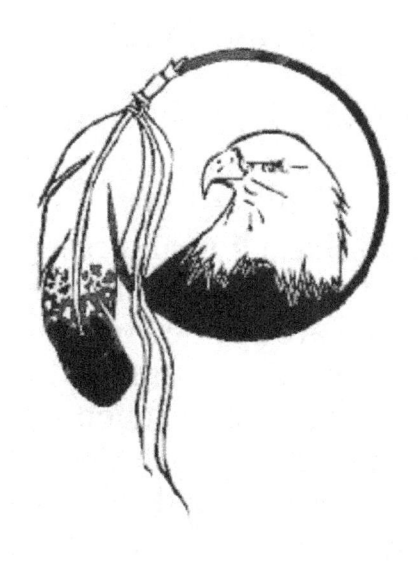

*"THE SPIRIT OF THE LORD IS UPON ME,
BECAUSE HE ANOINTED ME TO PREACH
THE GOSPEL TO THE POOR.
HE HAS SENT ME TO PROCLAIM RELEASE
TO THE CAPTIVES,
AND RECOVERY OF SIGHT TO THE BLIND,
TO SET FREE THOSE WHO ARE OPPRESSED,
TO PROCLAIM THE FAVORABLE YEAR OF
THE LORD."*

The Good Fight

Brothers, we ought not to be fighting one another.
Who is the true enemy here? Look within and you will see him,
Roaming about like a lion and ready to devour!
He is eating us alive, this enemy –
Because we are blinded by our pride!
It is time to forgive, and contend for our faith,
Together to stand, fight the enemy face to face!
Take up our full armor which Creator provides,
Not run off like cowards and seek places to hide!
Did our Creator not Himself face the enemy for us?
In our pride or in Creators Word – where shall we place our trust?
For the enemy is very real! He is powerful and strong!
But not as Mighty as our Warrior King to Whom we all belong!

Beloved, when I gave all diligence to write unto you of the common salvation, it was needful for me to write unto you, and exhort you that ye should earnestly contend for the faith which was once delivered unto the saints. For we do not wrestle against flesh and blood, but against principalities, against powers, against the rulers of the darkness of this age, against spiritual hosts of wickedness in the heavenly places. Therefore take up the whole armor of God, that you may be able to withstand in the evil day, and having done all, to stand. Stand therefore, having girded your waist with truth, having put on the breastplate of righteousness, and having shod your feet with the preparation of the gospel of peace; above all, taking the shield of faith with which you will be able to quench all the fiery darts of the wicked one. And take the helmet of salvation, and the sword of the Spirit, which is the word of God; praying always with all prayer and supplication in the Spirit, being watchful to this end with all perseverance and supplication for all the saints— Fight the good fight of faith, lay hold on eternal life, whereunto thou art also called, and hast professed a good profession before many witnesses.

The Mighty Little Warrior!

Some didn't listen.
He was after all, a mere child.
What wisdom would exist truly,
In such a small spirit?
Ah! Small but mighty!
For Great Spirit had come
To visit this little one
In the early morning light!
Small wonder, filled with Wisdom
And Light! And Power from above!
But nobody listened.....
And yet he continued to press on
Doing what he had been called on to do,
To lead men into the light
And out of the darkness....
If only they knew!
And then one day it happened,
That the Light of Great Spirit
Shone out beyond the limits of
What men had come to know!
And the Mighty Little Warrior danced
Before the crowd that day,
And as He danced in Great Spirits Power
Men fell on their knees and prayed!

And it shall come to pass afterward, that I will pour out my spirit upon all flesh; and your sons and your daughters shall prophesy, your old men shall dream dreams, your young men shall see visions: And also upon the servants and upon the handmaids in those days will I pour out my spirit. And I will shew wonders in the heavens and in the earth, blood, and fire, and pillars of smoke. The sun shall be turned into darkness, and the moon into blood, before the great and the terrible day of the LORD come. And it shall come to pass, that whosoever shall call on the name of the LORD shall be delivered: for in mount Zion and in Jerusalem shall be deliverance, as the LORD hath said, and in the remnant whom the LORD shall call. The wolf also shall dwell with the lamb, and the leopard shall lie down with the kid; and the calf and the young lion and the fatling together; and a little child shall lead them.

What Time is It?

Watch yourselves
For the Light is fading,
The light of His Mercy and Grace!
There is only a short allotment of time
Which He measures for all to do right.

Do not take for granted
His dawning of days,
For one day He's returning
And will take them away.
He won't listen to excuses then,
Or give out one more chance.

What time is it friend?
At your watch would you glance?
We know not when He'll come,
Perhaps today's the last chance ...

(For he saith, I have heard thee in a time accepted, and in the day of salvation have I succoured thee: behold, now is the accepted time; behold, now is the day of salvation.)

Raising Warriors of Faith

How will we answer our children one day,
When they ask why we allowed them to go astray?
Why we didn't tell them about Jesus,
Or share with them His Word?
What kind of answer from our lips will be heard?

Heavenly Father, help us do this right!
To raise our young Warriors to Battle in Faith!
To teach them of Love and Your Mercy and Grace,
And raise them to be honorable and walk in Your Strength!
Help us Creator, before it is too late!

I will open my mouth in a parable: I will utter dark sayings of old: Which we have heard and known, and our fathers have told us. We will not hide them from their children, shewing to the generation to come the praises of the LORD, and his strength, and his wonderful works that he hath done.

Dancing in Glory

You do not walk in vain, My Warriors!
Though on the journey there is pain!
Loss and tears, and fears relieved!
Keep moving forward! Do not be afraid!

Have I not told you I'm preparing a place?
Something new, as I promised for the whole human race!
Keep moving forward! Keep your eyes on the Prize!
Soon shall you see your good Faith come to life!

Now you know in your heart!
You have not seen, yet you believe!
Keep moving forward
As you draw nearer to Me!

Do you notice on your journey
That My Voice is getting clearer?
My Spirit within you stronger?
Louder roars the mighty river?

Stay close to one another Warriors!
Continue to encourage one another!
For you are all My Warriors!
You are all sisters and brothers!

Hang on to your crowns!
You shall be dancing in Glory!
Do not grow tired and faint!
Soon shall be the Grand Entry!

After these things I looked, and behold, a great multitude which no one could count, from every nation and all tribes and peoples and tongues, standing before the throne and before the Lamb, clothed in white robes, and palm branches were in their hands; and they cry out with a loud voice, saying, "Salvation to our God who sits on the throne, and to the Lamb."

Behold! Our Victory is Nigh!

We will not be afraid!
Though the tempest may come,
Shouting in our ears!
Why should we falter?
For Creator is with us!
Has He not promised
To always be near?
Behold! He is coming!
Rising upon the tempest!
Shout now our Victory cry!
His Warriors appear!
Fearless and Brave!
For He gives us HIS ARMOR
To battle the enemy
Which shall fall to his knees!
The Warriors cry out!
'Glory to Our Creator!
Which has come to our aid,
To set all captives free!'

Now I saw heaven opened, and behold, a white horse. And He who sat on him was called Faithful and True, and in righteousness He judges and makes war. His eyes were like a flame of fire, and on His head were many crowns. He had a name written that no one knew except Himself. He was clothed with a robe dipped in blood, and His name is called The Word of God. And the armies in heaven, clothed in fine linen, white and clean, followed Him on white horses. Now out of His mouth goes a sharp sword, that with it He should strike the nations. And He Himself will rule them with a rod of iron. He Himself treads the winepress of the fierceness and wrath of Almighty God. And He has on His robe and on His thigh a name written:

*KING OF KINGS AND
LORD OF LORDS.*

Who Are We Following?

Who are we following?
If we are following a visionary,
Where did they get the vision?
If we are following a teacher,
Where did he get his degree?
There are many drawing followers
Who are leading Warriors astray!

We should be careful who we follow!
Even a preacher might deception be giving!
We should follow only Jesus Christ,
For He is the One who bled and died
To raise up from the grave for us!
And arose up into Heaven!
He isn't serving stale bread
Which is poisoned with insincere leaven!

The one who walks in front of you
May look good on the surface,
But you shouldn't put your faith in any MAN!
Only Creator is the way to find purpose!

For no one else besides our Lord
Can offer the drink to quench our thirst!
There's only ONE way to gain Eternal Life,
Who you follow will determine
If you live or die!

Beware of false prophets, which come to you in shee p's clothing, but inwardly they areravening wolves. Ye shall know them by their fruits . Do men gather grapes of thorns, or figs ofthistles? Even so every good tree bringeth forth good fruit; but a c orrupt tree bringeth forth evilfruit. A good tree cann ot bring forth evil fruit, neither can corrupt tree bring forth good fruit. Every tree that bringeth not forth good fruit is hewn down , and cast into the fire. Wherefore by thei r fruits ye shall know them.

Emanating Light!

They called him a savage.
They did not understand
That within his heart he held the Power
Which Great Spirit had hidden there.
They looked upon him
As though he were a spectacle,
Something to amuse themselves with,
A source of entertainment.
But when he danced
The Power within him arose
And radiated out of him
Like the rising of the sun!
And so they came to watch him dance,
But walked away wondering
What it was about him
That had made such an impression.
... and so they sought the Light themselves.
To him it did not matter
Just what the people thought,
For when he danced
He only danced for an audience of ONE,
And that is how the POWER was released
To change the hearts of those
Who left his presence forever changed!

Ye are the light of the world. A city that is set on an hill cannot be hid. Neither do men light a candle, and put it under a bushel, but on a candlestick; and it giveth light unto all that are in the house. Let your light so shine before men, that they may see your good works, and glorify your Father which is in heaven.

The Edge!

The enemy would confuse me,
Pulling me in different directions,
Upset the balance – no foothold –
Knocking me off balance
To try to bring me down!
NO! Creator, I will not listen!
For Creator is not the author of confusion!
HE will not give me different instructions
From what He has already given –
Given in The Sacred Scriptures!
Herein there is balance and strength
To give to me the edge
Over the evil schemes of the enemy!

For God is not the author of confusion, but of peace, as in all churches of the saints.

The Lifter of My Head!

The enemy would have you looking down,
And in your shame to have you bound
Up with chains of his own design –
For Creator took Your place and died
To set you free from this downward spin
Lift up your head to look at Him!
Where is this thing which was your sin?
It died at Calvary, and was buried in Him!
Arise! My soul! Arise and sing!
Hope yet in God! See now He comes
To lift you up from off the ground!
Newness of life in Him is found!

Why art thou cast down, O my soul? and why art thou disquieted within me? Hope in God: for I shall yet praise him, who is the health of my countenance, and my God. But thou, O LORD, art a shield for me; my glory, and the lifter up of mine head.

A Higher Calling!

No matter how hard this trail gets
I shall not give up my hope!
I shall not waver in my Faith
In Creator's Mighty works!
For He has seen me through the fire,
And through the raging sea,
And He leads me to a better place
Remaining faithfully with me!
Weary I may grow, and yet
I shall press on ahead,
No matter what life throws my way,
Or how rough the going gets!
'Be not afraid! For I am with you!'
Creator whispers in my ear,
'Keep going child, I have provided
The way to bring you near!'

I press toward the mark for the prize of the high calling of God in Christ Jesus. Let us therefore, as many as be perfect, be thus minded: and if in anything ye be otherwise minded, God shall reveal even this unto you. Nevertheless, whereto we have already attained, let us walk by the same rule, let us mind the same thing. Brethren, be followers together of me, and mark them which walk so as ye have us for an ensample. (For many walk, of whom I have told you often, and now tell you even weeping, that they are the enemies of the cross of Christ: Whose end is destruction, whose God is their belly, and whose glory is in their shame, who mind earthly things.) For our conversation is in heaven; from whence also we look for the Savior, the Lord Jesus Christ: Who shall change our vile body, that it may be fashioned like unto his glorious body, according to the working whereby he is able even to subdue all things unto himself.

Lead Them!

My Warriors, I have sought you out,
But Your Creator has a purpose
For all men to come to what I've revealed
Unto you! Would any man be worth less?
And so as I lead, will you lead too?
My footsteps mark the path so clearly!
Now go my tender Warriors, Go!
Now lead your brothers near Me!

And he said unto them, Go ye into all the world, and preach the gospel to every creature.

For All of the Pain of Life Unfair

For all of the pain of life unfair,
Do not harbor resentment.
Creator says, 'Seek not revenge!
For I am coming to avenge!'
Behold! Heaven opens!
Behold! A white horse!
And who is its rider?
He's 'Faithful' and 'True'!
Fear not! O Warriors,
Weary from the trail!
He is coming in righteousness,
His Goodness shall prevail!
Ride calmly on, His Victorious Warriors!
Hold your heads up high!
He's comes to establish His Perfect Order!
For all of the pain of life unfair . . .
Our Great Warrior Chief shall meet us there!

And I saw heaven opened, and behold a white horse; and he that sat upon him was called Faithful and True, and in righteousness he doth judge and make war.

You Are Not a Door-mat!

I have called you to share
My Saving Message everywhere!
But if those you're sent to do not agree,
Then My Warriors, I set you free!

Warriors, you are not a door-mat
Upon which men can wipe their feet!
Remember this as you are sharing
My Saving Message with those you meet.

So take these Precious Pearls I've given
But do not cast them before the swine!
Yet love the lost, pray for them always,
As it is for these I chose to die.

So go in Peace, and love the love-less,
To set the sin-bound captives free!
But please remember this, My Warriors,
YOU are first Most Dear to ME!

Give not that which is holy unto the dogs, neither cast ye your pearls before swine, lest they trample them under their feet, and turn again and rend you.

I Can Do All Things Through Him!

I'm glad that I never gave up the struggle.
I'm glad that I always tried.
Even though at times I felt
Like throwing in the towel.
I'm glad that I was hard on myself,
I'm glad that I never heard
The voice of doubt who whispered to me,
Even when the whisper grew loud.
I'm glad that I walked past all the jeers,
Ignoring whoever was cruel.
I'm glad that instead I counted on Christ,
Who told me that I could!

I can do all things through Christ who strengthens me.

The Work of My Hands!

Be who I made you!
Not what society wants you to be.
Your Creator has placed you, and made you unique.
Society would change you, steal your identity.
Your identity in your Creator so vast and distinct!
And that I have called you to dance to My beat!
Amazing! Perplexing! But that's WHO you ARE!
Not pagans, not refuge – but MY SHINING STARS!
So go now My Warriors! You're marked for My Work!
And as you enter My Circle know that I danced there first,
To show you the way, and to teach you the steps,
And painted you beautiful with My Own Fingertips!

Always,
Your Creator

I will praise thee; for I am fearfully and wonderfully made: marvellous are thy works; and that my soul knoweth right well.

Sometimes You Will Have to Dance Alone

My Child,
Sometimes you will have to dance alone.
Do not be afraid.
Remember that you are My Own,
And this shall always be!
There will be times when those whom you trust
Will walk away from you.
But my Child, just keep dancing!
For I am watching you!

At my first answer no man stood with me, but all men forsook me: I pray God that it may not be laid to their charge. Notwithstanding the Lord stood with me, and strengthened me; that by me the preaching might be fully known, and that all the Gentiles might hear: and I was delivered out of the mouth of the lion. And the Lord shall deliver me from every evil work, and will preserve me unto his heavenly kingdom: to whom be glory for ever and ever. Amen

The Spirit Came Down

When I was talking to Creator,
And I came with a humble heart,
Creator met me in the shadows
His Spirit to impart.
I could not stand still for a moment,
For His Spirit bid me, 'Rise!
Now dance for Me, My little Warrior!
I shall watch you with My Eyes!'
And as I danced before Creator
The shackles fell off one by one,
And before I knew I was dancing freely
In perfect union with The Son.
I cannot say that I am perfect,
For I'm a lame, old wounded horse,
But for the Mercy in His Spirit,
I now can dance and keep the course!

The Spirit of the Lord is upon me, because he hath anointed me to preach the gospel to the poor; he hath sent me to heal the brokenhearted, to preach deliverance to the captives, and recovering of sight to the blind, to set at liberty them that are bruised.

The Sacred Feather

Jesus held it first, The Sacred Feather.
Men marveled at how Creator was moved by His Prayers.
His Warrior braves asked Jesus to teach them how to pray,
And this is how the Sacred Feather came to exist for us today.
There's Power in the Words of Prayer, and in Cries of the Heart,
But Praise to our Creator is where this Power surely starts!

And it came to pass, that, as he was praying in a certain place, when he ceased, one of his disciples said unto him, Lord, teach us to pray, as John also taught his disciples. After this manner therefore pray ye: Our Father which art in heaven, Hallowed be thy name. Thy kingdom come, Thy will be done in earth, as it is in heaven. Give us this day our daily bread. And forgive us our debts, as we forgive our debtors. And lead us not into temptation, but deliver us from evil: For thine is the kingdom, and the power, and the glory, forever. Amen.

Resting

I grew weary on the trail,
And so I found a place to rest.
There on the rough and weary journey,
I found a spot to lay my head.
I did not feel the bitter howling
Of the wind as it blew by,
I only knew the calm assurance
Of my Creator as he was nigh.
How can the God who made the mountains,
And made the oceans vast and wide,
Care so much for such a sinner
And wounded spirit such as I?
And how can the God who placed the stars
Within the sky, each in its place
Find the time to come from Heaven
To enlighten this bitter human race?
How can a God righteous and holy
Turn my sins as white as snow?
And keep and guard me as I journey,
And keep me company as I go?
I do not understand His Love
For me as sorry as I am.
I only know that for His Warriors
Our blessed Creator has a plan!

Sioux Couple

What is man, that thou shouldest magnify him? and that thou shouldest set thine heart upon him?

Where Does Your Help Come From?

*I will look up!
Where does my strength come from?
Not the mountain!
It is but made of stone!
The river cannot help me!
Nor the trees made of wood!
Not the sky, nor the valley
Do me any earthly good!
But to bask in His creation
No matter where my life leads,
I will look up to The Maker
Of all of these things!*

*I will lift up my eyes to the hills—
From whence comes my help?
My help comes from the Lord,
Who made heaven and earth.*

What Darkness?

His Light dispels the darkness.
He finds me in the night,
and turns the tide to calm assurance,
all shall be all right!
I soar on wings of Eagles,
His Spirit stirs me on,
Great Spirit lifts me up on high,
by His Strength I'll carry on.

Arapahoe Tipis in camp

For God, who commanded the light to shine out of darkness, hath shined in our hearts, to give the light of the knowledge of the glory of God in the face of Jesus Christ.

Bricks of Struggle

Bricks are hard, their edges sharp,
Like trials hard to take;
To stack upon one another and
Struggle to create a shape.
The mortar used to glue them fast
Is often mixed with tears,
And often we will have to wait
For the mortar to set for years.
A ton of bricks upon us borne,
Don't drop them or they'll break,
Instead lay each and mortar tightly
And painstakingly to create
Your life! Stand back and see with pride
What your trials in life have built!
See how strong your life is now
From bricks of struggle still?

Arikara Family

But I am poor and sorrowful: let thy salvation, O God, set me up on high.

Are We There Yet, Dad?

"Are we there yet, Dad?
How much longer will it be?
I'm getting tired of the journey,
You're not being fair to me!
Are you listening, Dad?
Can we stop and take a break?
Dad, are you sure you got the right directions,
Could you have made a big mistake?"

And Father smiles, and nods His Head,
Saying, "We'll be there soon enough!
Hang on a little longer, Child!
I know the waiting's tough!"

For when we were yet without strength, in due time Christ died for the ungodly.

Burying Injustice

Sorrow, you must stay behind me now.
What happened once between us best forgotten.
I shall keep the memories sweet tucked in my heart,
But the bitter gall of injustice done I choose to bury now . . .
So sorrow stay behind me, and I shall move ahead,
Without you at my heart eating away at every bend.
History shall not repeat itself once more,
On this most sordid part of me I choose to shut the door.
Forgetting that which I have left behind,
And pushing on toward better things
By Creator's Grace somehow.

Brethren, I count not myself to have apprehended: but this one thing I do, forgetting those things which are behind, and reaching forth unto those things which are before!

What We Bury . . .

Father of my heart I give
To You all that I have,
My hopes, my dreams,
My love of life –

Use it all as You have planned!
Through tears of loss,
And tears of joy,
And of gratitude and pain.

Father I confess that I
Cannot fathom Your ways,
What I am giving to You now
Is not what of You I prayed.

I prayed for blessing Father,
But now You send me rain?
Yet I shall trust in Who You Are,
And give to You my praise!

For my loss within Your Hands is life!
What I bury in this tomb
Is bigger than what I understand,
And shall become a brighter bloom!

When the Sabbath was over, Mary Magdalene, Mary the mother of James, and Salome bought spices so that they might go to anoint Jesus' body. Very early on the first day of the week, just after sunrise, they were on their way to the tomb and they asked each other, "Who will roll the stone away from the entrance of the tomb?" But when they looked up, they saw that the stone, which was very large, had been rolled away. As they entered the tomb, they saw a young man dressed in a white robe sitting on the right side, and they were alarmed. "Don't be alarmed," he said. "You are looking for Jesus the Nazarene, who was crucified. He has risen! He is not here. See the place where they laid him. But go, tell his disciples and Peter, 'He is going ahead of you into Galilee. There you will see him, just as he told you.'" Trembling and bewildered, the women went out and fled from the tomb. They said nothing to anyone, because they were afraid.

How Long, O Lord?

Waiting on Creator . . .
In the midst of this trial.
Exhausted from the journey,
I have walked many a mile
In circles? It often seemed to be,
Lost then found, perplexed inside of me,
Over and over and now I've stopped
With strength enough to call on my God!
Waiting . . . but I don't like to wait!
Patient . . . not my greatest trait!
Believing . . . in what I cannot see!
Trusting . . . in His will for me!
And in this process of slowing down,
Finally silent to stand my ground
In Faith! Creator lifts me up!
Praise God my Eagles Wings are found!

But they that wait upon the LORD shall renew their strength; they shall mount up with wings as eagles; they shall run, and not be weary; and they shall walk, and not faint.

Hardened

There are times when I feel hardened by life.
Put on my stoic face and go through the motions,
Don't cry – don't feel – don't accept what's real –
Push down deep within the emotions.

Creator comes along side of me,
My Counselor and Friend,
And makes me face what has made me hard,
'NO! I do not want to see!'

~ And Yet His Finger is pointing
At what my heart is most avoiding,
I must face and forgive the most annoying
In order to gain His Blessed Anointing!

For unto us a child is born, unto us a son is given: and the government shall be upon his shoulder: and his name shall be called Wonderful, Counselor, The mighty God, The everlasting Father, The Prince of Peace.

Don't Give Up!

Don't give up, O Faithful warriors!
Do not give up before it's done!
For only those who persevere
Can finish the race and claim the cup!
What of disappointment? Failure?
Arise! Dust off! Get back in the race
To run for Him, not looking back!
There are no prizes for
Those who are slack!
See there ahead?
The clouds are parting!
See there His Light?
IT SHINES FOR YOU!
To lead you through this start to finish!
Your Warrior God shall guide you through!
Your Warrior God shall guide you through!

Therefore we also, since we are surrounded by so great a cloud of witnesses, let us lay aside every weight, and the sin which so easily ensnares us, and let us run with endurance the race that is set before us, looking unto Jesus, the author and finisher of our faith, who for the joy that was set before Him endured the cross, despising the shame, and has sat down at the right hand of the throne of God.

Wounded Pride

I was trying to show off
In front of my Father.
'Watch me, Dad!
Did I make you proud?'
Father smiled, He waved His hand
To acknowledge me
Just where I stood.
And as my pride
Puffed up my longing
To allow my works
To be seen of men,
I stumbled in the dance,
Dis-heartened,
And hurt my pride
Where I did land!
I looked up somberly to see
If Father still was watching me.
He was! Oh! How embarrassed
I felt there as I
Massaged my skinned up knee!
And as my wounded pride stared laughing
I looked up to see my Father's Hand,
Which helped me to my feet! Imagine!
Loving me though I was not 'all that!'

Pride goeth before destruction, and an haughty spirit before a fall.

Watch and Wait!

Oh! How I want to be there
When His trophies He hands out!
I want to hear Yeshua when He
Gives the Victory shout!
'Well done, My good and faithful servant!
Look here, I have your crown!'
What better goal to keep in mind
As we stand upon this troubling ground?
So watch for Him, my brothers!
Stay strong in Him and wait!
Let's watch together for His appearing!
Our God is never late!
NO! Our God is never late!

Henceforth there is laid up for me a crown of righteousness, which the Lord, the righteous judge, shall give me at that day: and not to me only, but unto all them also that love his appearing.

Warriors on a Mission

Stand strong! Stand tough!
With a constitution of iron!
Hard as nails, innocent as doves . . .
For you shall be hated because of Me.
Just as I was also hated because of you!
Hated for hanging out with sinners,
And supping with the hookers –
Those were my friends in the hood!
'You claim to be God, and yet look!
Hanging out with those no-goods!'
Ah! Yes, religious people –
I've had enough of them!
But here you must remain,
Living amongst them until I return –
Warriors on a mission –
A Mission for God!
Are you up to the task?
I know that you are!
For my Spirit within You
Shall lead you far,
Far and wide to win souls for Me!
Stand strong, My Warriors,
For I stand with Thee!

Be on your guard; stand firm in the faith; be courageous; be strong. If you do not stand firm in your faith, you will not stand at all.

To Whom is the Arm of the LORD Revealed?

There was a time when I was so weak,
So vulnerable and small.
I was nothing – hopeless –
Without a place –
Without sustenance –
Lost –
Crawling on the ground in the dirt,
A lowly worm . . .
What happened then?
It's remarkable!
Unthinkable!
Mind blowing!
Miraculous!
That Creator would have even
Stooped so low
As to touch me
And bend me,
Bend me as to break me!
And there where I was broken
Emerged a set of wings so stunning,
I scarcely could believe it!
Then, then He came
And breathed HIS OWN SONG into me!
Unbelievable, you say?
But wait!
See where you are broken?
Your wings are emerging!

Who hath believed our report? and to whom is the arm of the LORD revealed? For he shall grow up before him as a tender plant, and as a root out of a dry ground: he hath no form nor comeliness; and when we shall see him, there is no beauty that we should desire him. He is despised and rejected of men; a man of sorrows, and acquainted with grief: and we hid as it were our faces from him; he was despised, and we esteemed him not. Surely he hath borne our griefs, and carried our sorrows: yet we did esteem him stricken, smitten of God, and afflicted. But he was wounded for our transgressions, he was bruised for our iniquities: the chastisement of our peace was upon him; and with his stripes we are healed.

A Rock and a Hard Place

I was stuck between
A rock and a hard place.
I was all cried out.
What was I to do?
I began to praise –
Praise Creator for all of His many blessings –
Praised Him for the storm –
Praised Him for His Merciful forgiveness
From hitting this rock – to before I was born!
That is when the Light began to dawn,
When He had me backed into this spot!
Shining His Light on all that HE IS,
And all the things I'm not!

From the end of the earth will I cry unto thee, when my heart is overwhelmed: lead me to the rock that is higher than I.

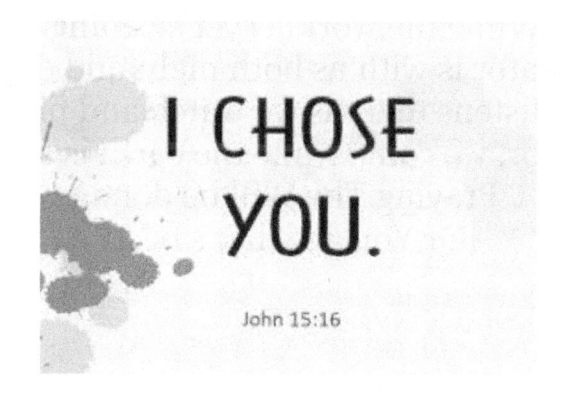

I CHOSE YOU.

John 15:16

Night Watch

Praying in the night – our calling –
To pray without ceasing
Through the night hours
While the world is yet sleeping.
Creator is with us both night and day,
He listens to us as we watch and pray!
Creator, we come while the earth is at rest
Praying Thy Will be done,
For You do what's best!

Yet the LORD will command his loving kindness in the daytime, and in the night his song shall be with me, and my prayer unto the God of my life.

Purpose

This heavy load I carried,
The glitter and gold of struggle
To attain the wanting stilled at last,
Bitter weight borne in my past!
Pride! Prideful ways, Creator!
Wanting to be seen and heard!
But within a loneliness obstructed,
My heart's desire still disturbed!
Those heavy weights borne on my shoulders!
For what, Creator? I ask You now!
For gladly You would bear this burden,
And give me solace! Would You now?
So I will gladly lay the burden
Down before Your feet at last!
To find my burden light as a feather,
To ease the struggle of the past!
Forgiveness found! Life's bitterness within me gone!
I place my hand upon my chest,
Where Creator's Heart echoes His Drum!

Come unto me, all ye that labour and are heavy laden, and I will give you rest. Take my yoke upon you, and learn of me; for I am meek and lowly in heart: and ye shall find rest unto your souls. For my yoke is easy, and my burden is light.

Why Can't We Fly?

'Why can't we fly, Creator?
What is it that's holding us down?
Could it be all the weight of indifference?
And the bitterness we keep in our hearts?
What makes it so easy for You to rise up?
Are we not to be rising with You?
You tell us to pick up and endure the Cross!
But it's so heavy! Now what do we do?'

"This is a mystery, My Warriors!
How did this work for me?
As I carried the Cross I forgave in my heart!
See? This is how you set your wings free!"

….. so now we pray – 'Help us Creator!
'Not my will, but Yours be done!
And forgive those who have hurt us Creator,
For they know not what they've done!'

And you hath he quickened, who were dead in trespasses and sins; Wherein in time past ye walked according to the course of this world, according to the prince of the power of the air, the spirit that now worketh in the children of disobedience: Among whom also we all had our conversation in times past in the lusts of our flesh, fulfilling the desires of the flesh and of the mind; and were by nature the children of wrath, even as others. But God, who is rich in mercy, for his great love wherewith he loved us, Even when we were dead in sins, hath quickened us together with Christ, (by grace ye are saved;) And hath raised us up together, and made us sit together in heavenly places in Christ Jesus: That in the ages to come he might shew the exceeding riches of his grace in his kindness toward us through Christ Jesus. For by grace are ye saved through faith; and that not of yourselves: it is the gift of God: Not of works, lest any man should boast. For we are his workmanship, created in Christ Jesus unto good works, which God hath before ordained that we should walk in them.

The POWER of HIS NAME!

When will I know?
How will I know?
Is there an end to this circle,
This circle of life?
Around every bend a heartache will touch us,
And push us to bend or to break.
I will not break!
I stand stoic and proud!
God has me firmly planted,
And rooted on high ground!
When will I know?
Perhaps it does not matter ...
For what good would it do me
To know when my end shall be?
Perhaps it is better to live long and free . . .
Knowing that Creator is with me ~
~ Ah yes! This shall be enough!
Enough to keep on dancing
Despite the struggle and the 'rough' –
Smooth out the edges?
Ah! How would that work?
If I did not lean on Creator
To help me through the 'hurts'?
For they Glorify His Name!
Yes! They Magnify His Name!
And show within my weakness still
The POWER OF HIS NAME!

And he said unto me, My grace is sufficient for thee: for my strength is made perfect in weakness. Most gladly therefore will I rather glory in my infirmities, that the power of Christ may rest upon me.

My God Stands Guard!

I do not fret at what is behind me.
I only move forward, His Hand to guide me.
He's got my back! I shall not fear!
Wherever He leads me, My God is near!

Thou hast beset me behind and before, and laid thine hand upon me.

Foot-prints

Will I leave prints, Creator?
Will what I have been leave the way
Marked and clear for my brothers to follow?
Oh! I pray Creator! Please give me the courage
To tread where I fear to tread!
To walk the way of our people
And leave a trail behind!
Not a trail of tears, Creator!
Our people have had enough tears!
But rather a trail of Light, Creator!
Light to carry them through the years!
What will You say, Creator,
When all is done? Shall You bid me come?
Shall You bid me enter in
As a Faithful Servant of Your Son?
May my feet leave marks upon the spirits
Of every man I touch in life!
Marks that lead them to Your side
There where the end is found to strife!

How beautiful upon the mountains are the feet of him that bringeth good tidings, that publisheth peace; that bringeth good tidings of good, that publisheth salvation; that saith unto Zion, Thy God reigneth!

Wounded Warrior

He mourned the stripes which life had given,
The beatings which were unfair.
And every time he dreamt to venture
Forward, they were there
To knock his dream down a notch or two,
To tell him that he was a failure,
And so embittered from the fight
He gave up his life's endeavor.
What stripes for him His Savior bore,
Such as were so unfair!
His crying eyes looked up to see
Not his Savior but his own body there.
'For me, Creator?' he asked in shame?
'Yes! For you, My wounded warrior!
None other could bear these stripes for you,
So I took your place right there!'
… and so with one last ounce of courage
He set himself back up on his feet,
And vowed to his Brave Creator once more
To overcome his life's defeat!

And David was greatly distressed; for the people spake of stoning him, because the soul of all the people was grieved, every man for his sons and for his daughters: but David encouraged himself in the LORD his God.

Tears for the Mortar

Could the tears build a bridge to wholeness?
Could the memories be bricks with which to build?
Could the longing within me be broken
With a Promise that's kept? Better still
To know without a shadow of doubting
That better days are up ahead!
This is what after all You have promised
Within the Sacred Scripture of Yours I have read!
... and so I keep building one brick at a time,
My tears used to mix up the mortar to stack
Up on brick at a time on this bridge toward tomorrow,
The bridge closing the gap to the past!

They that sow in tears shall reap in joy.

Thy Rod and Thy Staff

This valley is forever it seems,
But I am a Warrior on a mission!
Creator told me to walk this path,
And so I'm going to stay right with it!
Does that mean that His Warriors don't get tired?
That we don't get fussy once in a while?
Of course not! And He understands!
(If only we could look at His big smile!)
And yet though I walk through this valley,
Full of shadows which frighten me to death,
I am not going to fear any evil! NO!
For Creator walks with me every step!
His rod and His staff, they comfort me!
And when I grow weary of the burdensome miles,
I draw even closer to my Creator then,
And just lean on Him for a while!

Yea, though I walk through the valley of the shadow of death, I will fear no evil: for thou art with me; thy rod and thy staff they comfort me.

Division in the Ranks

You should be so bonded,
That you are one in spirit!
Joined together in unity!
So tightly knit that no enemy
Could break the bond you have!
So much one in heart
That one of you alone could not fall!
So why are we falling?
Why are we falling short of the mark?
Did I not say that each of you
Was a member of the body?
Why are there some members running off
Getting into mischief and folly?
……… get it together My Warriors!
For things are about to get ugly!
I wasn't just blowing out hot air
When I said tribulation was coming!
I didn't ask that you jointly
'Stay awake now and pray!'
So that you would ignore it
And each walk separately away!
Come! I am calling out to my Warriors now,
To come together in peace
And walk together somehow!
Do not neglect one another,
The end is coming with precision!
For the enemy is wise, My Warriors!
And he feeds on division!

But exhort one another daily, while it is called To day; lest any of you be hardened through the deceitfulness of sin. And let us consider one another to provoke unto love and to good works: Not forsaking the assembling of ourselves together, as the manner of some is; but exhorting one another: and so much the more, as ye see the day approaching.

Are We Walking in The Light?

Are we walking in the Light, my brothers?
Are we gathered in a good way?
When we are blessed to be together,
Do we together pray?
For the day is growing shorter, brothers!
The final moon shall soon arise!
Are we walking in the Light, my brothers?
Are we 'seeing' with our eyes?
If we are fighting one another,
Then Creators Blood was shed in vain!
Are we happy in our 'Family'
Which is called by Creator's Name?
... THE SPIRIT TELLS US CLEARLY
That IF WE LOVE ONE ANOTHER WELL,
The BLOOD OF JESUS CHRIST WILL CLEANSE
OUR SINS – the sins of ONE AND ALL!
Are we walking in the Light, my brothers?

But if we walk in the light, as he is in the light, we have fellowship one with another, and the blood of Jesus Christ his Son cleanseth us from all sin.

Children of the Red Earth Gather

Children of the red earth gather.
We carry the flag with pride,
The flag that symbolizes yet
The death of our brothers still.
The flag we died to protect,
Even those who once had despised us,
For this is the Way of Creator!
Forgiveness – and life for all people!
Great Spirit in us taught us His Ways
Long before the war began.
We shared HIM with our children as
The red earth fed us from her hand.
And so with pride we gather still
To Praise Creator for the rain!
The rain which comes to wash away
The pain of what has been!

Trail of Tears, California State University Long Beach

But I say unto you, Love your enemies, bless them that curse you, do good to them that hate you, and pray for them which despitefully use you, and persecute you; That ye may be the children of your Father which is in heaven: for he maketh his sun to rise on the evil and on the good, and sendeth rain on the just and on the unjust. For if ye love them which love you, what reward have ye? do not even the publicans the same?

Jesus walks on water, by **Ivan Aivazovsky**(1888)

In My Human-ness

As a storm of life prevailed still,
Without the thunder rolled,
And I felt lost within its noise
Beyond human control!

And yet He came to visit me!
Yes! Walking on the waves!
'My Warrior, I know you're afraid!
Have You called Me? Have You prayed?'
'Creator! I was sore afraid!
Just looking at the storm!
I thought that You were sleeping!
Yes! I did not call Your Name!'

'Come Warrior! Walk upon the waves!
But keep Your Eyes on Me!
Pay no mind there, though the thunder roars!
Walk toward Me as You Pray!'

I made a bad decision then,
To take my eyes off of Creator,
And underneath the waves I fell,
Doomed to drown as sure as ever!

…but there appeared His Steady Hand
To pull me from this mess!
'My Warrior! Why did you ever doubt?'
Appeared my human – ness.

Once more I trod the wicked waves,

       To keep my eyes on Creator still,
And Heard Creator command the storm,
       'Now settle! Peace be still!'

And Peter answered him and said, Lord, if it be thou, bid me come unto thee on the water. And he said, Come. And when Peter was come down out of the ship, he walked on the water, to go to Jesus. But when he saw the wind boisterous, he was afraid; and beginning to sink, he cried, saying, Lord, save me. And immediately Jesus stretched forth his hand, and caught him, and said unto him, O thou of little faith, wherefore didst thou doubt?

There's a Storm a 'brewing...

There's a storm a 'brewing ....
Look up ahead!
Can you feel it in the air?
The sky! I said to watch it!
Are you watching it now?
The cold is moving in quickly!
Do you feel it in the hearts of men?
The falling away has begun, My Children!
There's less of you, and more of them!
Make up the camp! Stand guard and watch!
It's time for you to pray!
Pray and keep each other strong
While it is called to-day!
And watch My Warriors!
Watch the sky!
For there are changes in the air!
I will return, though you know not when,
But you better be prepared!

Watch therefore: for ye know not what hour your Lord doth come.

Believe

Borrowed Robes

This robe is not my own, but His!
For my own I could not clean,
For it was covered in the mirk and mire
Of all my forbidden sin!
On my own I was a wretched loss!
With no hope! Without a home!
So bleak was my misfortune then
That I could not call His Heaven Home.
But Creator came! To me? Oh yes!
To me and loaned me His!
His Very Robe of Righteousness
Which, did cover every sin!

I will greatly rejoice in the LORD, my soul shall be joyful in my God; for he hath clothed me with the garments of salvation, he hath covered me with the robe of righteousness, as a bridegroom decketh himself with ornaments, and as a bride adorneth herself with her jewels.

Thieves in Our Midst

Stay strong, My Warriors!
Endure temptation!
For you shall be tried and tested,
But you have My Word!

I am not a man that speaks
With forked tongue!
My Words are Life and Truth!
Believe it when I say to you
That you must overcome!

For there are thieves among you
Who will rob you of My blessings!
They will entice you ...
And their words will be sweet!

Entice you to break bread with them
As they twist My Words just so,
And many will fall victim!
So be careful where you go!

Remember your Brave Warrior King
Who endured to set you free?
My Warriors, He is with me now
Sitting to the right of Me!

And He is now preparing
For you all Your Victory Crowns!
But men will watch and wait to steal it
If you let your guard come down!

Hold fast to what you have in ME
So that they cannot rob you of your crown!

Blessed is the man that endureth temptation: for when he is tried, he shall receive the crown of life, which the Lord hath promised to them that love him. Behold, I come quickly: hold that fast which thou hast, that no man take thy crown.

Cry Babies!

Are we cry babies?
Are we always screaming loudly
Into Creators ear?

'We want this! We want this now!

Waaaah! Waaaah!
Give it here!'

Or are we content babies,
Waiting on Creator
Knowing that He will provide
Always, now – or later!

OR

Are we still stuck on milk
When we should now be
Eating meat?

Do we whine and carry on
Like spoiled brats
With each defeat?

These are things I ponder
As I'm looking at my life.
Will I be sleeping like a baby,
Or keep Creator up all night?

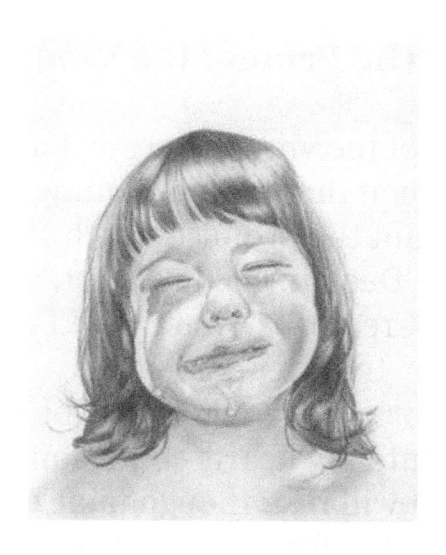

I have fed you with milk, and not with meat: for hitherto ye were not able to bear it, neither yet now are ye able.

The Fruit of the Vine

The fruit of the vine was ready for harvest,
And then there came a killing frost
To taint the promise which I held
Deep inside my heart.
'Why Creator? What now?' I cried,
In bitter disillusion.
Creator whispered, 'Peace, be still!'
Into my hearts confusion.
So I will rest, though faint I be
So hungry for that wondrous fruit!
Be it the fruit of love, of time,
Or sweet companionship – it was mine!
My dream! My heart's desire still!
And yet Creator, not my selfish will
But Thine be done! Though it be frost
Upon this fruit which I see as lost!

*Although the fig tree shall not blossom, neither shall fruit be in the vines; the labour of the olive shall fail, and the fields shall yield no meat; the flock shall be cut off from the fold, and there shall be no herd in the stalls: Yet I will rejoice in the L*ORD, *I will joy in the God of my salvation. The L*ORD *God is my strength, and he will make my feet like hinds' feet, and he will make me to walk upon mine high places. To the chief singer on my stringed instruments.*

Power Struggle............

I can feel it – the wind is shifting.
Do you feel it? It is moving us,
Moving us in a new direction
Away from the shadows and
Into The Light...

The night fades – can you sense it?
The night grows weaker day by day,
It's making room for The Light –
There is no place for shadows
In The Light!

Blinding! Oh! The Light is blinding!
To allow the wind to blow the scales
Off our eyes!
This shift in wind! His Spirit Blowing
Into hearts to melt the winter ice!

Now feel? The ground is shifting!
To shake the dust which settled on our feet!
Move now! The ground is shaking!
To move us ever nearer to His Feet!

Now bow! The Spirit's Power
To knock us down a notch or two He comes!
Acknowledge! There's no denying
The Power of His Spirit When He comes!

Then I arose, and went forth into the plain: and, behold, the glory of the LORD stood there, as the glory which I saw by the river of Chebar: and I fell on my face.

Forget Us Not!

Who are we, Creator?
Who are we to You?
Created in Your Image here
To work Your Perfect Will!
Who turned our backs upon You ourselves,
To Grieve Your Heart so, still....
And yet you think upon us Creator!
Why? We cannot fathom!
The very ones who drew first blood,
And yet You wouldn't forget us!

*I will not forget you.
I have carved you on the
palm of my hand*

Isaiah 49:15

What is man, that thou art mindful of him? and the son of man, that thou visitest him? ~ Can a woman forget her sucking child, that she should not have compassion on the son of her womb? Yea, they may forget, yet will I not forget thee. Behold, I have graven thee upon the palms of my hands; thy walls are continually before me.

Into The Light...

The night fades – can you sense it?
The night grows weaker day by day,
It's making room for The Light –
There is no place for shadows
In The Light!

Blinding! Oh! The Light is blinding!
To allow the wind to blow the scales
Off our eyes!
This shift in wind! His Spirit Blowing
Into hearts to melt the winter ice!

Now feel? The ground is shifting!
To shake the dust which settled on our feet!
Move now! The ground is shaking!
To move us ever nearer to His Feet!

Now bow! The Spirit's Power
To knock us down a notch or two He comes!
Acknowledge! There's no denying
The Power of His Spirit When He comes!

For this cause I bow my knees unto the Father of our Lord Jesus Christ!
If you died tonight, do you know where you would spend eternity?

Have you asked Jesus into your heart?

He's waiting to talk to you now . . .

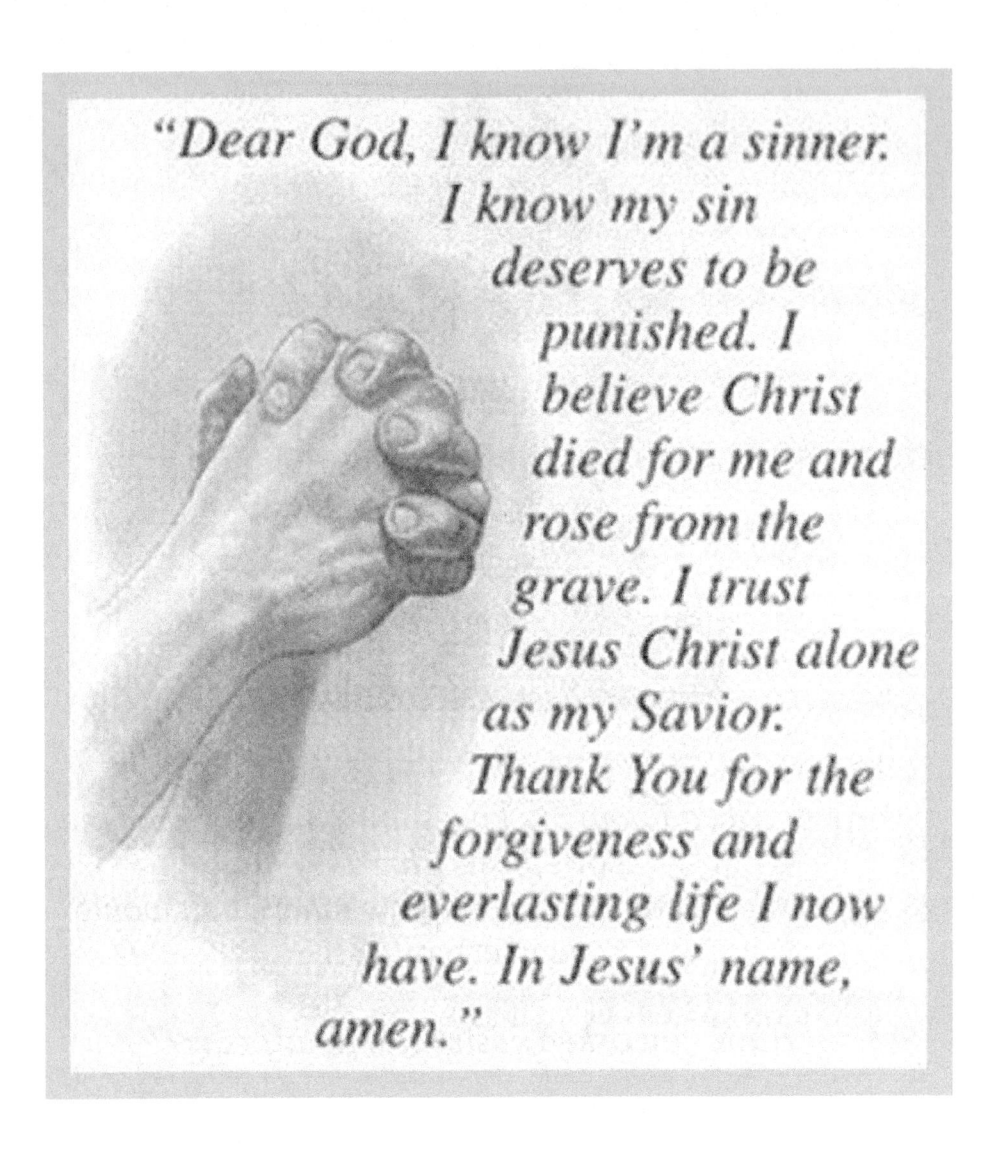

"Dear God, I know I'm a sinner. I know my sin deserves to be punished. I believe Christ died for me and rose from the grave. I trust Jesus Christ alone as my Savior. Thank You for the forgiveness and everlasting life I now have. In Jesus' name, amen."

Visit us on Facebook!

Hannah House Native American Outreach

http://hannahhouse2002.org/

Other books by Mary Bennett
AKA Dancing Dove

Available on Amazon.com
and
Barnes & Noble

In The Midst of Want

Awakenings

There Is A Tomorrow

When Autumn Comes

Forbidden Fruit

The Gifts of Dawn

Thorns Among The Roses

Warriors Of The Light

Ziv Productions & Publishers

Matthew 5:16

Hannah House
MPO Box 2813,
Niagara Falls, New York
14302